# AUSTRALIA'S SUBMARINER CHEFS

SCRAN

JOHN GOSS

Bayview Publishing

Copyright © 2025 by John Goss

All rights reserved.

No portion of this book may be reproduced in any form without written permission from the publisher or author, except as permitted by U.S. copyright law.

This publication is designed to provide accurate and authoritative information in regard to the subject matter covered. It is sold with the understanding that neither the author nor the publisher is engaged in rendering legal, investment, accounting or other professional services. While the publisher and author have used their best efforts in preparing this book, they make no representations or warranties with respect to the accuracy or completeness of the contents of this book and specifically disclaim any implied warranties of merchantability or fitness for a particular purpose. No warranty may be created or extended by sales representatives or written sales materials. The advice and strategies contained herein may not be suitable for your situation. You should consult with a professional when appropriate. Neither the publisher nor the author shall be liable for any loss of profit or any other commercial damages, including but not limited to special, incidental, consequential, personal, or other damages.

Book Cover by Bayview Publishing

Illustrations by Sandy Freeleagus

1st edition 2025

# Contents

| | |
|---|---|
| DEDICATIONS | IV |
| ACKNOWLEDGEMENTS | VII |
| PREFACE | 1 |
| INTRODUCTION | 3 |
| FEEDING A SUBMARINE CREW | 5 |
| FOOD HAPPENINGS | 10 |
| SUBMARINERS FOOD LANGUAGE AND DIET | 20 |
| RECIPE EXAMPLES | 28 |
| TERMINOLOGY | 41 |
| About the Author | 43 |

# DEDICATIONS

We humbly dedicate this book to all those submariner chefs who kept their crews alive and worked miracles in a galley no bigger than a small garden shed.

To all those listed below, this book in the Submariner Chefs Register and to those who may yet to come or be registered as a Submariner Chef we salute you for your dedication and skills

**Quote, RAN Cookery Manual, ABR 5 of 1970:**

> *"The way people satisfy hunger and appetite from day to day has a direct effect upon their well-being. It also influences appearance, moral and attributes to others. The moral fibre of the whole crew can be affected by the meals."*

# AUSTRALIAN SUBMARINER CHEFS

# REGISTER 2025

In the early days the chefs were known merely as Cooks, but in more recent times there qualification have been recognised and thus they now deserve the recognition of Chef.

## AUSTRALIAN SUBMARINER CHEFS

Allen, R A
Anderson
Arnold, James
Badenoch Billy
Bailey R
Barker J
Bellman Dave
Beresford Patrick
Birch C
Broughton R
Button DJ
Callander Brett
Carman Sam
Carroll M
Cashion, Grant
Christie, Stuart
Clarke, Don

Coathup Rick
Conlon Steve
Daniels J
Dansey P
Day J N
Day, Jamie
Delaney Peter
Elliot
Farmer
Fishwick Crystal
Gilchrist JJ
Gilmour SN
Gilshenen Barry
Goss John
Gurr John
Halstead Kevin

Hawthorne Richard
Healy, Michael
Hetherington J
Horan B
Jones Peter
Kasch Dereck
Kenney Sean
Kenny D
Lee J
Lever M
Linnane, Thomas P
Lloyd, Clive
Masterson Michael
McCall, Michael
McGuigan
Metcalf, Jean Paul
Morley Bruce
Mundry Gene
Murner V

## AUSTRALIAN SUBMARINER CHEFS

Newson AJ
O'Beirne John
Ollett M
Pardoe M
Power AS
Rinderman, Gary
Ross S
Rowell S.B.
Rowley Terry
Ryan Collin
Scanlon Des
Seaton JM
Shaw D
Sheehan Peter
Simmonds. John

Singer Tomer
Skinner Greg
Smith A
Stepetz M
Stephens Mitchell
Stone B
Sweeney M
Taylor Brad
Walsh G
Wilkinson Grant
Young Ray

*Oberon Submarine leaving Sydney Harbour*

# ACKNOWLEDGEMENTS

**Ex Leading Chef Greg Skinner** — for his insights and assistants with the recipes as adapted for submarines and his assistance with research in assembling this and previous the previus edition

Greg joined RAN 1970 as junior recruit and served on HMAS *Queenborough* as an ordinary seaman. He completed his cook's course in 1972 and was drafted to HMAS *Albatros*s, the Naval Air Station at Nowra. He subsequently served on the aircraft carrier HMAS *Melbourne* between 1972-1974 and joined submarines in 1975 where he served on HMAS *Oxley* and HMAS *Otway*.

I also acknowledge:
- Royal Australian Navy – Recipes for 50, 1986 Cookery Training Section Manual, HMAS *CERBERUS*

- Pat (One Chop) Beresford for his assistance

- Sandy Freeleagus for his wonderful cartoons and art work

- Thor Lund for compiling and editing this and previous books for me.

- Bayview Publishing for their support and sponsorship.

# PREFACE

The challenges for food service personnel on board our earlier submarines will be somewhat different for the next generation of submariners with the boats being much larger, spacious, and a better living environment for the projected increased crew size from 65 to around 140. My time started as the RAN introduced the submarine capability into the fleet in the early 1960's, based out of Sydney at HMAS *Platypus* on the north shore of Sydney harbour.

My first experience of submarines came straight out of the Cookery School at HMAS *Cerberus*. With minimal practical cooking experience in June 1967, I headed off for Royal Navy Submarine training in UK HMS *Dolphin* in Portsmouth. I was then posted to HMS *Odin* out of Submarine Base in Faslane Scotland.

Recalling the time: cold war and lengthy submarine patrols off the vast western coastal regions of Russia was an extremely tense period for the world. Planning for a patrol period of around 6 weeks plus an extra 2 weeks for contingency, a crew of 65, 3 meals a day with no Supermarkets around the corner made it difficult to say the least. Bringing supplies onboard in a sequenced manner allowed chefs to follow a menu based on starting from the front and eating your way to the back. This made for some interesting menus. Food choices on RN submarines were based on simplicity with ration supplies such as dehydrated veggies, tinned sausages and powdered products such as milk, potato and egg as part of our on-board provisions.

To complicate matters, the Royal Navy Cooks at the time had to contend with the stowage of rum, cigarettes and beer. The second storage problem, which the Cooks had to consider on RAN submarines, also was beer ut not rum. The submarines carried a stock of 200 cases of cans of beer to satisfy the daily beer issue of "two cans per day per man per day" *at the CO's discretion*. Officers usually preferred gin or brandy. The RAN was not prepared for submarine victualling which led to early problems with space and handling It took several years of fighting the system, both within Navy and Defence contracting, to finally acknowledge the issues of submarine storage.

The recognition of the catering skills that many was also a problem. I was very proud, that after setting the wheels in motion around 1981, our Defence Force Caterers now receive commercial training and receive Certificates of Proficiency to support their work options once they leave the Defence Force. Our submarine Chefs will always be revered by those who served in boats and I expect the tradition of excellence will continue with the current and future submariner chefs.

> **Note**: The recipes included in this book come from the 60's and 70's and do not refllect the current cuisine on current submarine fleets.

*Oberon Class Submarine*

# INTRODUCTION
## AUSTRALIA'S OBERON CLASS SUBMARINES

The Royal Australian Navy's First Submarine Squadron consisted of six Oberon Class Submarines: an initial order of four and a second order of two.

The Oberon class of submarines were in service in the RAN from 1967 to 2000. The six "O" boats: HMAS *Oxley, Otway, Ovens, Onslow, Orion,* and *Otama,* were all based at HMAS *Platypus* in Neutral Bay, Sydney, until the submarine squadron moved to HMAS *Stirling* in Western Australia.

The operational endurance of these Submarine often included many weeks at sea, and it fell to two sailors from the catering branch, usually a leading rate and an able seaman, to provide four meals a day for a crew of 60+ sailors. This places significant pressure of the Cooks to apply their skills to create nutritious and attractive foods.

When the stock of fresh food items was reduced, they had to resort to the stocks of frozen, dehydrated, tinned, and powered produce. Making bread also became a daily task once the fresh bread runs out, and this could extend their workday to 16/18 hours every day for their time at sea which could be up to 4-5 weeks.

*Typical Oberon Submarine Galley*

*Leading Cook Greg Skinner in action*

# FEEDING A SUBMARINE CREW

Storing for a patrol began with the taking on of victuals; when the miniscule sized fridges and the dry store were full, extra stores were stacked and lashed out of the way in the forends (Torpedo Compartment) and in extreme cases anywhere that can be found like under bunks. A small proportion of the crew were day workers, outside the system of four watches; these included the cooks who worked tirelessly to keep the food coming and the variety interesting.

There is only one galley in a Submarine, and the same food is provided to everyone. Four meals a day were served; breakfast, lunch, dinner, and a midnight snack when the watches changed. Early in the patrol when fresh vegetable were available, meals were good, but as the patrol progressed and fresh vegetable disappeared, the Cooks were obliged to produce appetising meals from frozen meat and veg or from tins. It was not unknown for the crew to be placed on restricted meals as the victuals ran out. Sweet biscuits were a much-treasured delight and carefully rationed.

All meals were eaten in the individual messes, which could make life difficult for those living in the aft mess. To collect your meal, you had to travel through the motor room and engine room, passing though the control room and through three watertight bulkheads. The trip was made more difficult if the engine room, motor room and control room were getting ready to snort (to run the diesels while under water) and the control room was in "red lighting" with all the lights switched off.

# FOOD LOGISTICS

Victualing/Food Allowance: When considering a weekly menu, the Cooks with the Coxn had to factor in costs against the ingredients of each dish. A Fixed Issue Price List (FIPL) was provided and updated annually. Additionally, an allowance was calculated against each member attending the meals.

An example of this rate was $1.60 per man per day throughout the 1970's. Items not listed on the FIPL would be calculated at their purchased cost price. Hence, fillet steak was an unlisted FIPL item and when taken into consideration against the daily allowance the cost would blow the daily budget out of the water. This practice was abandoned in the 1980's.

Storing a submarine for a long patrol was an art. The crew of 60+ needed to be fed four times a day. That can be around 8,000 meals over a long patrol. Getting the food on board and down through the hatches was an unenviable heavy work task that required precision storage and handling.

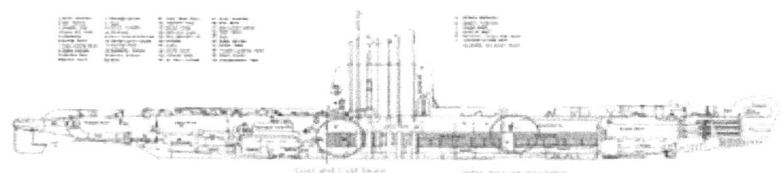

*Circled are the food storage areas including dry stores under the galley and aft is the frozen food storage and nearby vegetable storage*

**All frozen food** was stored in a freezer just aft of the control room. to access the freezer, you had to remove a steel hatch, go down a ladder to enter the cool room where fresh fruit and veg were stored. Behind the cool room was the freezer. The Engineering Officer would only allow you to go down into the freezer and cool room twice a day to get the food that was needed for that day.

**Other fresh vegetables** were kept in AMS next to the Radar Office below the Control Room.

**Dry stores** were held in a compartment below the Galley accessed by a hatch in the main passageway. At times this could be dangerous and was not done during busy times.

**On long patrols**, canned and other non-perishable food was stored in the forends (Torpedo Compartment). It was often a major task to work out how much was left, and how to portion it out to the end of the patrol.

## OBERON SUBMARINE MESSDECKS

Meals were prepared in the galley and transported to the messdecks by hand. Officers had a steward and Senior rates a Messman and the Tankee to deliver the ordered meals. The Messman and Tankee were assigned from the crew and notionally, the senior rates messman came from the engine room staff whilst the Tankee who assisted Chefs with provisions came from the forends crew and reported to the Coxn. Officers had a Steward to serve them and look after their needs. Depending on the boats position, either surfaced or dived, eating a meal could be a challenge at times if the weather was rough on the surface or during steep angles when dived.

*Typcal Oberon Submarine messdeck where meals were eaten when bunks were folded*

*Typical Oberon Submarine Junior Sailors Forward Mess. Note the bunks convert to seats for meal time*

# AUSTRALIA'S SUBMARINER CHEFS

# FOOD HAPPENINGS

## INTRODUCTION

There are many stories and myths around submariners' food habits and victualling. We have gathered a few of the stories we've heard from those that were there and seem to be more truth than myth. These stories will give you a look into the often rebellious and off-beat nature of submariners from the Oberon eras. The language is sometimes a bit fruity, but it was that way back then, so we have kept it as near as possible to the terms and language used without wishing to offend any readers.

## FORK IT

Next to the galley in the passageway leading to the forward mess there was a large hatch that was used to gain access to one of the submarines battery compartments. Electricians would climb into the narrow crawl space through this hatch to test the batteries at certain times during the day and night. A certain Messman exiting the Chiefs and Petty officers mess, tripped and dropped a metal fork down the open battery compartment hatch when a greeny (electrician) was down there taking dips. According to the messman he never saw a greeny move that quick before.

## SURFACING SHORTBREAD

It seemed like a good idea to one Chef or maybe the steward to use up all the existing flour before they headed back to port and an opportunity to give the crew a treat of freshly baked shortbread biscuits after a long-submerged passage. Having placed the trays in the oven and setting the temperature, the chef headed forward to watch the movie and duly fell asleep after a long hard day. With the galley and the boat filling with smoke an emergency surface was declared with the boat surfacing. It was rumoured that some stoker (engine room person) managed to find a couple of not too badly burnt biscuits and was seen munching on them whilst the rest went over the side. The chef wasn't punished formally, but the galley needed a lot of work, and this was completed alongside before the Chef went on leave.

## TRIMMING BREAD

A bread company produced a 'special' bread mix so that submarines could bake fresh bread at sea. The Chefs' meticulously followed the recipe; the bread came out of the oven. It looked like bread, it smelt like bread but it weighed like lead. The loaves were totally inedible. The rumour goes that a certain Trimming Officer even piped to move two loaves from for'ard to aft to balance up the trim.

*Victualling ingenuity*

# COXSWAINS SURPRISE

A certain Coxswains discovered that after an unplanned flood all the tinned food in the lower part of the store had been flooded, and the labels washed off. Not to be defeated he ordered the chefs to do what they could with the unlabelled cans rather than ditch them. It became known as Cox'ns' Surprise and was documented as follows in a lyrical way.

**Ingredients,** Unmarked cans of stuff, Tin(s) of arri's (Arrigoni's), Sauces of any type but Tomato preferred, Large pot.

Find all the tins of stuff in the bilges where the labels have washed off or the tins have been damaged. Avoid the engine room stored unmarked tins. Pour the unmarked tins into a large pot. It doesn't matter what it is as the occasional can of fruit is ok with the meaty stuff. Bring to a boil, thrown in the arri's (tinned tomatoes), salt and pepper. If it smells a bit off, just add curry powder till it smells better and change the menu to Coxn's Curry Surprise. If you have them, throw in a few raisins or currants and call it Coxn's Sweet Curry Surprise.

**Note**: *Serve with mouldy Penicillin bread or Polly crackers. Be aware, there can be some side effects from poorly selected, mixed ingredients.*

## BILTONG STEW

A certain Coxn bought several large cans of something called B'Tong Beef whilst in transit via South Africa. It looked chunky and smelt alright, so it was cooked with herbs and spices and served. However, it was as tough as hell and gave everyone the runs. We still don't know what it was, but some believed it was canned Wilder beasts Stew that he bought. There were no seconds on this unusual dish and most of it went over the side into the Indian Ocean.

## ROUGHERS

When the weather got too rough to dive and cooking too hazardous or impractical, those not on watch turned into their bunks and, in some cases, strapped in to avoid falling out of their bunks. As the crew still had to eat the chefs would open and heat tins of stew and other stuff and place them in large metal pots. These were then pushed or carried to the crew to eat in their bunks. Given the narrow space in the crew bunks it was often quite a task to digest the food in a prone position and spillage was often the result.

## MEAT CORRUPTION

A certain supplier to the submarine squadron was falsifying his meat deliveries to the boats by under packing and falsifying the stamped weight on the cartons. The actual shortfall wasn't discovered until the boat was at sea and the meat cartons opened. This was discovered by one Cox'n who had been a victim of the fraud but rather than initially taking the usual naval supply chain action (which happened later) the store ship sailors formed a special ops team who took his truck whilst he was being entertained in the junior sailor's mess and had it driven to a local park and left open with a sign free meat, help yourself. Needless to say, when the truck was recovered it was empty and smelt to high heaven having been left open for some days. The locals enjoyed the free meat and its rumoured some sent thank you notes to the provider.

## NEW RECIPES TESTED

A certain chef had been watching a TV Chef call Graham Kerr who was very popular at the time. The Chef decided to try one of Kerr's spicier recipes on the crew whilst at sea. The crew loved it but the aftermath was not pleasant on the nose, and the flatulence in a confined space was intolerable.

*Crew emission concerns*

## RED DICK REBELLION

A certain Cox'n found he could save a few dollars by increasing the number of meals that involved Frankfurt's (red Dicks). The crew had other ideas. Whilst storing for the next patrol, under the watchful eye of the Coxn, the store ship party slipped every second box over the side into the bay. We often wondered what the fish made of it.

**The Red Dick Song:**

(Sung to the tune of 'The Sound of Angry Men'
From Les Miserables).
Do you hear the sound begin
It is the sound of angry men
They're sitting down for scran and it's Red Dicks again;
Oh you bring us to our knees,
Can you tell us Cox'n, please
What would it take to serve a steak or chops.
We've had Red Dicks in a stew,
We've had them boiled right through,
We've had them under pastry and served up as a pie,
And even though it hurt,
We've had 'em with custard for dessert,
And I wouldn't recommend the deep fat fry.
The Stokers and the Greenies while storing ship down aft
Whenever a box of Red Dicks went over the side they'd laugh
There's many a box of Red Dicks in Neutral Bay.
We had them as a curry
Don't try that again in a hurry,
Then we went all Chinky - an' had 'em sweet n' sour
And the smell was quite ripe
When he mixed them in with tripe,
They shouldn't have put in all that cornflour.
Do you hear the sound begin
It is the sound of angry men
As they sit down for scran expecting to be fed;
That Cherokee Love Dart
Is aimed right at our heart,p
So Cox'n please will you victual in the red.

## TANKEE'S STILL

The story goes that a certain Tankee found a way to ferment potatoes in a seldom visited part of the AMS to make a rather potent spirit out of it. The problem came with filtering the brew, but this was solved using women's panty hose. The game was discovered when the perpetrator washed the panty hose and hung them in the engine room to dry. Despite a lot of creative excuses, a certain officer doing rounds discovered a female emerging from the AMS after hours with a bunch of sailors following. It did not go well for those on board but thankfully no one drank any of the liquid which was disposed of quietly and the still dismantled.

*Refit capers*

## THE CUSTARD CREAM BISCUIT AFFAIR

One Tankee noted that the engine room staff had found a way into the sweet biscuits in his store. The shortbread custard cream biscuits were a much-treasured prize. It appeared that whilst inspecting something mechanical within the Tankee's store, packets of these delicacies found their way into the tool bags, and then went aft to the delight of the stokers. Once discovered, it led to a ban on unescorted access to the store and suspension of the biscuit issues to the aft mess.

## THE CASING BARBEQUE

*Submariners Barbeque at sea underway*

It was common practice on long surface passages for the crew to have a Barbeque on the casing. A small gas fired barbeque would be set up between the forward Hydroplanes which were stored vertically on the surface and deployed horizontal when diving. This made an ideal place for the barbeque and a canvas swimming pool that was occasionally set up in tropical climes. The Chefs often took time off from cooking whilst crew members cooked for them. These were wonderful events, and a chance to get some fresh air and bond with the crew members from other parts of the boat. The shape and design of the newer submarines appears to preclude that experience.

## POTATO PEELERS DERBY

Watchkeepers in the forends were often given the task of peeling the potatoes for the next day's meals. It appears that the potato peeler derby started when one watch-keepers proudly displayed a 1 metre long continuous potato peel. It wasn't long before his record was broken as others took on the challenge. The competition even saw the introduction of shore bought special peelers and other home-made devices. The competition ended when the number of spuds peeled diminished as competitors spent more time finding the perfect spud and carefully peeling it. Betting was also part of the competition which led to some animosities and disputes and brought an end to the activities.

## BAGUETTE SPEARS

A well-meaning Coxn made a shore purchase of fresh bread baguettes thinking the crew might like some fresh bread after a long passage to a foreign port. However, the first day back at sea, the baguettes were stale, and jokes ran around the boat about the Coxn's secret weapon, and some wag drew a diagram explaining the loading routines to put them into the tubes. One Chef decided to see if he could save some of the baguettes by soaking a couple in milk and water then baking them in the oven for a short period. He quickly discovered that whatever they were made of it certainly wasn't a type of flour that he was used to and the smell from the oven was more like baked sewerage. They all went overboard and are probably still floating around out there somewhere.

## COFFEE WITH A SLICK

Coffee was the brew of choice by most submariners trying to stay upright and awake through long hours with little rest. The problem of contaminated coffee came about when the large coffee tins were opened and the foil seal was removed. Putting the lid back on firmly didn't fully seal the can in most cases with the coffee dust therein exposed to the ever-pervasive diesel fumes. The additions of hot water created coffee with an oily slick on the surface. Strangely enough submariners became used to the taste and some had trouble enjoying untainted coffee when they got home.

*Dieso coffee offset*

# SUBMARINERS FOOD LANGUAGE AND DIET

Meals or Scran as it's known took on somewhat of an event to be looked forward to at times. However, you had to know what was being served and to the uninitiated the language of food for submariners was confusing. Train smash, Burgoo, Excreta ala Kon tiki, Babies' heads, and so on confused the unfamiliar and scared many of them at their announcement whilst the submariner met them with delight or derision.

Many of the names for the dishes came from the submariners who trained in the UK with the RN. Many are no longer politically correct. It is difficult to believe that submariners not only ate some of the more exotic concoctions developed in desperation by the creative Chefs but looked forward to it. The eating process was always a challenged in the cramped confines with the smell of diesel and unwashed bodies and clothing. Smoking was common also in those days so heavy haze for mealtime was often the case. Chefs food hygiene requirements called for them to shower more often than the rest of the crew.

- Adam and Eve on a raft = 2 eggs on toast or fried bread
- Apples (i.e. pint of) = cider
- Arrigoni's = Tinned Tomatoes
- Baby Spew = Sandwich spread
- Ballet Dancer Shit = strawberry angel delight
- Banjo = egg filled roll
- Burgoo = Porridge
- Chicken On a Raft = Egg on toast
- Chinese wedding cake = rice pudding
- Cows egg = milk
- Elephant's toenail = pastie
- Elephants Trunk = Sliced Spam
- Fullers earth = pepper
- Goffer = fizzy drink
- Harbour cotters = bread slice of fish like a giant fish finger
- Kye = hot cocoa drink
- Mermaids' piss = Vinegar
- Moo juice = milk
- Nellies Wellies = elephants footprints
- Dark Dick = Sliced Black Pudding
- Droppings in the snow = baked rice pudding with raisins

- Periscope Cheese = large tin of processed cheese

- Piss filters = Kidneys

- Rats coffin = pastie

- Shit on a raft = Devilled kidneys on toast

- Skinheads on a raft = Beans on toast.

- Sneeze = Pepper

- Snorkers in fearnought = battered sausage.

- Spithead pheasant = Wardroom slang for kippers

- Texas strawberries = baked beans

- Train smash = Arrigoni's (tinned tomatoes) and sausages at worst the tinned type or rashers of bacon.

- Yellow Peril = Smoked Haddock

- Cheese ush = cheese flan

- Woolly beef= lamb Frog in a bog = toad in the hole

- Pot mess = meat and veg stew in a 6-gallon pot

# TYPICAL FIRST WEEK AT SEA MENU

### Monday

**Breakfast** – ashore before slip and proceed

**Lunch** -Roast Lamb/Pork, Baked Potatoes, Peas/Pumpkin/Carrots/Gravy,

**Dinner** -Chicken Maryland / Beefsteak Pie. Mashed Potato, Corn, Grilled Tomato, Crumbed, Pineapple.

**Dessert**-Apple Pie & Custard

### Tuesday

**Breakfast** -Scrambled eggs/Fried eggs/Crumbed Lambs' brains (Babies heads) bacon,

**Lunch** - Grilled Rump Steak/ Chicken Curry & Rice, Chips, Peas/Corn/Cabbage,

**Dinner** - Beef Casserole (Pot Mess)/ Veal Schnitzel & Gravy, Boiled Potatoes, Beans /Carrots/ Mixed Veg.

**Dessert**- Rice pudding

### Wednesday

**Breakfast** -Poached /fried Eggs, Bacon, Lambs Fry,

**Lunch** - Spaghetti Bolognaise/ Roast Chicken & Gravy, Roast Potato, Roast Pumpkin, Peas/Carrots,

**Dinner** -Sweet and Sour Pork with Rice/ Grilled Beef Rissoles, Chipped Potatoes, Beans/Carrots /Corn.

**Dessert** - Prunes & Custard

### Thursday

**Breakfast** -Scrambled Eggs/Fried Eggs, Bacon, Bubble & Squeak,

**Lunch** -Grilled Lamb Chops/ Chilli Con Carne & Rice, Mashed Potato,  Mixed Veg, Peas/Corn,

**Dinner** Crumbed Fish / Beef Curry & Rice, Lyonnais Potato, Peas/Carrot/Pumpkin

**Dessert** -Bread & Butter Pudding

### Friday

**Breakfast** Poached Eggs/Boiled Eggs (Bum Nuts) Bacon, Kidneys (Piss strainers)

**Lunch** -Pot Roast of Beef / Chicken Chow Mien & Rice, Roast Potato, Pumpkin, Peas/Beans,

**Dinner** - Corned Silverside (Corned Dog)/ Baked Pork Chops, Mashed Potato, Carrots/Beans/ Cabbage

**Dessert**-Apple Crumble & custard

### Saturday

**Breakfast** – Omelets/ Fried Eggs, Tomato au Gratin (Train Smash)

**Lunch** - Hungarian Beef/ Sausages & Gravy, Boiled Potato, Mixed Veg/Beans/Carrots,

**Dinner** - Baked Savoury Meat Loaf/ Egg & Bacon Pie, Lyonnais Potato, Peas/Cabbage/Carrots

**Dessert**-Jellied Fruit & Ice cream

### Sunday

**Breakfast** - Fried Eggs/Poached Eggs, Bacon, Savoury Mince

**Lunch** - Fried Fillets of Fish/ Shepherd's Pie, Chipped Potato, Beans/Grilled Tomato/Corn,

**Dinner** - Baked Leg of Ham/ Beef in Black- bean Sauce with Rice, Boiled Potato, Mixed Veg/Beans/Cabbage

**Dessert**-Apple Crumble & custard and ice cream

## CONFUSING CIVILIANS

On the odd occasion that civilians were taken to sea for short periods on the submarine they would often need interpreters to tell them what the meal was. Some chefs took particular delight in this confusion by write up the meals in 'Submariner speak' as follows.

Breakfast – *Bum nuts or Train Smash*

Lunch - *Babies Heads or Elephant Foot*

Dinner - *Pussers Pot Mess or Coxn's Surprise*

Dessert-*Droppings in the snow*

Nine oclockers – *Kai*

No wonder many civilian passengers left a submarine with the impression that submariners were mad, but they never left unfed despite the weird names for the dishes and 'submariner speak'.

# RECIPES

The recipes that follow are from the 1960's and 70's and thus are no longer curent for todays submariners (thank heavens). You will note the quantities in most cases are set for 50 plus serves. The average Oberon submarine had a compliment of 60 plus, but often carried extra crew under training and occasionally civilians.

The language used is as it was back in those days, and some of the dishes were inherited from the Royal Navy. They have been included for the sake of accuracy, and that many Australian submariners endured the Royal Navy Submarine cuisine and some even enjoyed it.

*Never upset the chefs*

# RECIPE EXAMPLES

The following recipes were largely a hand down from the Royal Navy (RN), and picked up by our Royal Australian Navy (RAN) Cooks whilst undergoing their submarine training with the RN. The example dishes were served to our RAN Submariners throughout the earlier period of the Australian Oberon submarines service from the 1960's through to the 1980's. Thus, the following recipes do not reflect the changes to food schoices over Australia's Oberon's operations and certainly not the current submariner cuisine choices.

# Breakfast Favorites

### KIDNEYS ON TOAST – Piss Strainers on a raft

Ingredients – Yields 50

Ox kidneys 4.5 kg.
Stock 3 litres.
Pepper 2 teaspoons.
Fat for frying.
Parsley chopped ½ cup. Salt 2 tablespoons.
Lemon juice.
¼ cup .Flour 200 g.
Toast slices 50.

## Instructions

1. Skin kidneys, remove cores and cut into 15 mm dice. Fry in hot shallow fat until brown.

2. Add flour, mix until smooth, and cook two minutes. Add stock and seasonings, stirring constantly.

3. Bring to the boil, and simmer 20-30 minutes, or until tender.

4. Add lemon juice, and extra seasonings if necessary.

5. Serve on toast or fried bread, garnished with parsley.

Note - For variety, add 500 grams onions, finely chopped, and fried in   hot fat until brown, along with the stock.

# LAMBS FRY AND BACON - Animal Farm fry up

## Ingredients – yields 50

Lamb's fry, 5.5 kg.
Fat for frying.
Bacon rashers, 2 kg.
Flour, 200 g, Flour for rolling.
Stock, 3.5 lit.
Salt, 1 tablespoon.
Parsley, chopped, ½ cup Pepper, 1 tablespoon.

## Instructions

1. Skin lambs fry and cut into 5 mm slices.

2. Roll in seasoned flour.

3. Fry lightly in hot fat until brown. Lift into dishes and keep hot in a slow oven.

4. Add 200 grams flour to pan and mix with sufficient fat to make a smooth paste.

5. Cook 2 minutes, stirring all the time.

6. Add stock gradually, stir until boiling and simmer 5 minutes, stirring constantly.

7. Check seasonings. Cut bacon into even sized portions.

8. Arrange in overlapping rows in dishes.

9. Bake in moderate oven 7 minutes. Sprinkle lambs fry with parsley. Serve with bacon and gravy.

# Main Meal Favouites

## STEAK AND KIDNEY PIE

### Ingredients

Makes one individual steak and kidney pudding per person
Potatoes.
Gippers (Gravy) powder.
Carrots plus any green vegetable.
Stuffing mix.

### Instructions

1. Either boil or microwave steak and kidney pud, as per makers directions.

2. prepare and cook vegetables to suit.

3. Retain vegetable water, mix in gippo powder.

4. add a dessert spoonful of stuffing mix to thicken and to add flavour.

5. Either mash or serve potatoes whole.

Note - Taste before serving.

## ELEPHANT'S FOOTPRINTS

**Ingredients**

1 Tin of Spam.
1 Bowl of Batter.

**Instructions**

1. Slice Spam in quarter inch rings.

2. dip in batter & deep fry until crisp.

3. Serve with tinned peas and carrots.

## PUSSERS POT MESS OR CURRY

**Ingredients - Must all be from tins.**

2 Tins, Stewed Steak.
1 tin Potatoes.
1 tin Arrigoni's (Tomatoes).
2 tins mixed vegetables.
1 tin baked beans, cannellini beans, butter beans, or all three.
1 tin spaghetti.

## Instructions

1. Mix all together in large saucepan or pot, season to taste.

2. Cover, Heat very slowly on low heat, stirring occasionally, until festering.

3. Prior to serving add 1 tin of baked Beans, stir through and add extra heat.

4. Eat piping hot, with crusty bread from the fore-ends. (See also Penicillin bread).

Note – The ingredients of this dish are unlimited and to your own tastes. Best dished up in a mug, eaten with a spoon. For those of you who are now 'out of' the mess deck culture, soup plates will suffice! Can be added to, at will, with further ingredients to establish a 24-hour stock pot. Ideal for outward bounders/campers if you can keep it down.

# YELLER PERIL

## Ingredients

Haddock Fillets..
Milk.
Bread.

## Instructions

1. Fill a pan with some milk. The size of the pan and the amount of milk will depend upon the quantity of fish you wish to cook. Alternatively, UHT can be used if desperate. Do not use water alone, as it will pull the flavour out of the fish and attract more diesel smell.

2. Season with some pepper, Heat the milk. Do not boil the milk but heat it to just before boiling.

3. Add the haddock. Place the fish in the boiling milk, ensuring that they are covered in milk.

4. Allow the fish to simmer in the milk for about 10 minutes on medium heat. Check the haddock.

5. When the fish are done, they will have become completely opaque, and the meat should flake apart easily. If the fish looks translucent or pieces do not come free with a gentle tug, cook the fish a bit longer.

Note – Can be served at any time of the day as suits your crew. Use bread to mop up the milk sauce, yummo!

*Supplementing the menu*

# PUSSERS MUSHY PEAS

**Ingredients**

Dried whole Peas, (Now sold in 500 grams. Pkts.)
Bi carbonate of Soda. (Dessert spoonful)

**Instructions**

1. Half fill 3-4-pint saucepan with hot water.

2. Stir in the Bicarb, pour in as many peas as required, soak overnight.

3. Rinse well, a couple of times.

4. Cover peas with an inch or so of fresh water, salt to taste.

5. Bring rapidly to the boil, turn down to simmer and cover.

6. continue to simmer for 30-40 min. Ensure pan doesn't dry out, top up if necessary.

7. Drain, mash with good dollop of butter.

Note – white pepper & vinegar can be added during the mashing process also. Serve immediately with whatever you want. A superb accompaniment to Battered fish and chips. It has been known to make one pass wind. If served during a dinner party, blame the Dog!

## Dessert Favourites

# SPECIAL RICE PUDDING

**Ingredients**

One and a half 700gms of whole or small grain rice.
2 Dessert spoon Sultanas.
1Litre of milk.
Butter or Margarine.
Sugar.
Nutmeg.

**Instructions**

1. Put rice into pie dish.

2. Add generous tbsp. sugar, pour in milk.

3. Drop in Sultanas evenly.

4. Dot surface with shavings of butter or Marge.

5. Sprinkle evenly with Nutmeg.

6. Place on baking dish in a slow oven (300F) Gas 2, for 2 hours.

Note- Serve hot with Ice cream. Delicious cold mixed with jam.

# APPLE CRUMBLE AND CUSTARD

## Ingredients - For 4 persons

Large tin of sliced apple pie filling..
Grated rind of half a lemon.
1oz Caster sugar.
1 tin or packet of instant custard.

## TOPPING

- 6oz plain flour.
- 3oz margarine.
- 2oz caster sugar.
- 1oz Demerara sugar.

## Instructions – Pie

1. Arrange the apples thinly in a 3-pint pie dish.
2. Sprinkle with caster sugar, top with lemon rind.

## Instructions -Topping

1. For the topping, sieve the flour into a mixing bowl.
2. cut up the margarine and rub it lightly into the flour with the tips of the fingers.
3. Mix in caster sugar, spoon the crumble mixture over the apples and press it down lightly.

4. Sprinkle the demerara sugar on top.

5. place the dish on a baking tray and bake in the centre of the oven at 400 degrees F, Gas mark 6 for 45 minutes.

6. Heat up custard and pour over portioned crumble.

Note: This recipe can also be substituted with pineapple rings or rhubarb.

## PRUNES AND CUSTARD – Laxettives in yellow snow

### Ingredients – yields 50

Milk, 4.5 lts.
Custard Powder.
Tinned Prunes, 5 kgs.

### Instructions

1. Wash prunes in warm water.

2. 2.Bring milk to the boil.

3. Mix custard powder with water into a smooth paste.

4. Slowly pour into hot milk until thickened.

5. Add sugar and vanilla essence to taste.

6. Serve hot or cold with prunes.

# Beverage Favourites

# KAI

### Ingredients

One block of (preferably) chocolate, or any brand of cooking chocolate..
One tin Carnation milk
Boiling water.
Sugar if required.

### Instructions

1. Grate the block down using cheese grater, use 3 dessert spoons full per cup.

2. Pour in a small amount of boiling water.

3. Stir until chocolate is melted.

4. Add boiling water  continue stirring and top up with boiling water.

Note – enough to put hairs on anybody's chest! A grand pick-me-up.

# WATCHKEEPERS BREW

**Ingredients**

Coffee or tea
  Milk or Long Life
  Sugar to taste

**Instructions**

1. Put a large amount of Coffee or 2-3 tea bags in a dirty plastic mug.

2. Add a small amount of milk or Long life.

3. Stir into a paste.

4. Add boiling water

Note - Stand aside for an hour or so before drinking. Complain loudly and go and make another muttering as you go.

# TERMINOLOGY

For those not familiar with the language and terms used by submariners and sailors in days gone past we offer the following explanation of the terms used.

NOTE: Most quantities for recipes in this book are serves of fifty.

- Scran = meal or food

- Tanky = a sailor allocated to help the chefs and report to the Coxswain

- Squarie = Sailor's girlfriend till they marry

- Squeeze Guts – famous UK fast food outlet known to those in Dolphin 2

- Harry's = Harrys Café De Wheels, famous food truck near Garden Island Naval Base

- Targets = surface ships of any type

- Skimmers = surface ships sailors

- Deep fryer = submariner cook or the more rotund Deep fat fryer

- Seaweed suckers = submariners

- Whizzy = Worcestershire sauce

- Monkey spunk = vegemite or marmite for the British

- Blowies = sultanas

- Redders = tomato sauce

- Jimmy = Executive Officer (2<sup>nd</sup> In Command)

- Voice Pipe = method of communication between the bridge & helmsman when on the surface

# About the Author

John entered the Navy at 15 years of age. Following 12 months as a junior recruit he was posted to sea on HMAS *Derwent* and later HMAS *Anzac* before going the HMAS *Cerberu*s to complete his initial Cookery Course in 1966, on completion of his course he volunteered for submarines and went to the UK to undergo training as a submariner with the Royal Navy where he subsequently saw service on the Royal Navy Oberon class submarine HMS *Odin*. He later became part of the commissioning crew of HMAS *Ovens* and on return to Australia served on HMAS *Onslow*.

John progressed through the ranks in general service where he retired as a Commander in 2021. This book is the 3rd edition and has been a labor of love and dedication to his unique skills. The book is intended to highlight the often forgotten aspects of life at sea on a submarine during the Oberon era but also reflects the continued dedication and skill of the modern Collins class submariner chefs.

As John puts it " I enjoyed a full and exciting life in the Navy and wouldnt have changed a thing. Im sure some will find themselves in the pages of this book and I hope they enjoy those thoughts"

## Also by this Publisher

The Twilighters – Road Trip

Coffee Maidz – New Beginnings

BEBE – Finding Love

www.ingramcontent.com/pod-product-compliance
Lightning Source LLC
LaVergne TN
LVHW010304070426
835507LV00033B/3499